The DIVINE PHYSICIAN

DEVOTIONS FOR THE SICK

by William B. Ward

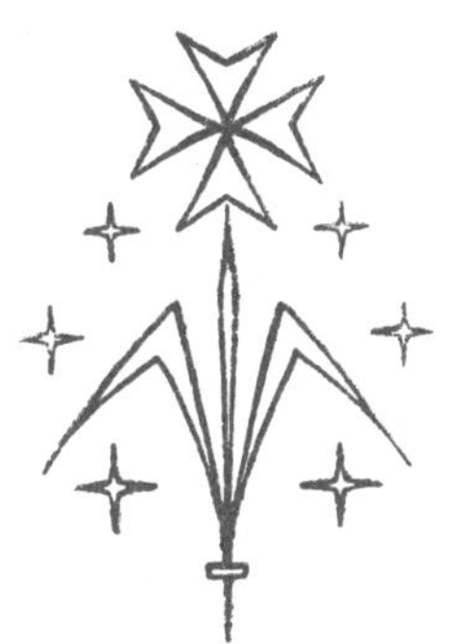

"And he healed many who were sick with various diseases."

(Mark 1 : 34, R.S.V.)

John Knox Press

ATLANTA, GEORGIA

Dedication

To my Mother, who served the Divine Physician as a nurse in the ministry of healing, and whose three sons now teach, preach, and heal in His name, this booklet is affectionately dedicated on her seventieth birthday.

Eleventh printing 1982

INTERNATIONAL STANDARD BOOK NUMBER: 0-8042-2316-5

LIBRARY OF CONGRESS CATALOG CARD NUMBER: 53-11762

Your Minister and You

Your minister considers it a high privilege to visit your bedside when you are ill. Read this sentence: "I believe the patient should send for his minister when he gets sick just as he sends for his doctor." That statement was written, not by a pastor, but by the physician who for years was chief of the Medical Staff of one of the country's largest hospitals.

The pastor's visit to you is a friendly call, and much more. He would minister to you the quiet peace, the cheerful faith, the inexhaustible healing power of God. His service is performed by his own personal interest and friendship, by giving "prescriptions" of appropriate verses of Scripture, and by the power of prayer.

Ministers are endowed with no sixth sense which enables them miraculously to discover when members of their congregations are ill. Some friend may tell your pastor of your sickness, or he may not hear of it. If he has not visited you he will appreciate your having someone call him, just as you would notify your physician.

If you belong to no church, or are in a strange city, your nurse will be glad to notify the hospital chaplain, or to call a minister of your religious preference for you.

1

The Divine Physician

WE USUALLY THINK of Jesus as a minister or preacher, but as we read the Gospels we see it would be equally true to regard Him as a medical doctor. He spent as much time healing as He did preaching. We read that people were brought to Him afflicted with divers diseases—leprosy, fever, palsy, epilepsy, withered hands, the blind, the deaf, the lame, and He healed them all.

In the Gospels we read such verses as "Jesus went about all Galilee, . . . healing all manner of sickness and all manner of disease among the people," and He "healed all that were sick: that it might be fulfilled which was spoken by Esaias the prophet, saying, Himself took our infirmities, and bare our sicknesses." (Matthew 4:23; 8:16-17.)

Once in the press of the crowd a woman who had been ill for twelve years came behind the Lord and touched the hem of His garment, crying in her heart, "If I may but touch his garment, I shall be whole." Immediately power came from the Lord, and the woman felt the glow of health pulsing through her body. The Master turned to see who had touched Him and said, "Daughter, be of good comfort; thy faith hath made thee whole." (Matthew 9:22.)

Though no longer with us in the flesh, Christ is still the Great Physician. We remember His words, "Lo, I am with you alway, even unto the end of the world." (Matthew 28:20.) Through the skill of the doctors, the care of the nurses, and the orderly processes of nature, His healing comes. By calm trust and faith we reach out and touch the source of all healing power.

> "But warm, sweet, tender, even yet
>   A present help is He;
> And faith has still its Olivet,
>   And love its Galilee.

> "The healing of His seamless dress
>   Is by our beds of pain;
> We touch Him in life's throng and press,
>   And we are whole again."

PRAYER

O Divine Physician, Thou didst walk the troubled ways of Galilee long ago, bringing health and peace and life. Give all who are ill today the consciousness of Thy presence, I pray. Let Thy power work through those who have given themselves to the ministry of healing in Thy name. May the tissues of my body respond to the unseen touch of Thy healing hands. In my heart I hear Thy words, "Be of good comfort; thy faith hath made thee whole." Amen.

The Power of Prayer

"The prayer of faith shall save the sick, and the Lord shall raise him up . . . Pray one for another, that ye may be healed. The effectual fervent prayer of a righteous man availeth much." (James 5:15-16.)

DR. ALEXIS CARREL, the physician who won the Nobel prize for suturing blood vessels and the Nordhoff-Jung medal for cancer research, calls prayer the most powerful form of energy that can be generated. He says the influence of prayer on the human mind and body is as demonstrable as that of the secreting glands. "As a physician," he wrote in a popular article, "I have seen men, after all other therapy had failed, lifted out of disease and melancholy by the serene effort of prayer. Only in prayer do we achieve that complete harmonious assembly of body, mind, and spirit which gives the frail human reed its unshakable strength."

Recently the author of this booklet of devotions suffered a severe illness in a distant hospital, which experience prompted the writing of these meditations. On the very day the sickness was most severe each family in the congregation was called and asked to hold special prayers for their pastor. Next morning the fever had abated, and the critical stage

of the illness was over. Some would call this a mere coincidence. But we who believe the world is governed by the
providence of an all-powerful Father find little room for a
so-called "mere coincidence."

Even in those times when it is not the Father's will for
prayer to heal, it can bring deep results to the spirit. One
man is embittered by cancer; another gains insight. One
man resents the encroachment of old age, while his neighbor
greets it as a bright destiny. The pain of arthritis makes one
a chronic grouch, and another a source of radiance. One
cannot accept death; another meets it as God's eternal plan
for the life everlasting.

> "More things are wrought by prayer
> Than this world dreams of."

PRAYER

Lord, teach us to pray, for we know that the secret of
abundant life is prayer. We ask for Thy healing power in
our bodies, and for Thy peace in our minds and hearts. We
thank Thee that Thou hast built the stairway of prayer, that
each of us may climb into Thy presence and find the answer
to our deepest needs in Thy redeeming grace. We pray in
Christ's name. Amen.

3

Peace Standing Guard

"And the peace of God, which passeth all understanding, shall keep your hearts and minds through Christ Jesus." (Philippians 4:7.)

THE NEW TESTAMENT Greek word translated "keep" means literally "to stand guard." It is a term from Greek military usage. When an army camped in hostile territory, at night one phalanx of soldiers stood guard around those who slept. Their overlapping shields made a solid wall of protection about the sleeping camp.

The peace of God stands guard about our hearts like a phalanx of soldiers, solid protection against any hostile worry or fear or tension which might slip through to attack us.

Jesus said, "Peace I leave with you, my peace I give unto you: not as the world giveth, give I unto you. Let not your heart be troubled, neither let it be afraid." (John 14:27.) "These things I have spoken unto you, that in me ye might have peace. In the world ye shall have tribulation: but be of good cheer; I have overcome the world." (John 16:33.)

In quietness and peace, Lord, I rest in Thy loving care. I surrender every anxious worry and apprehension unto Thee. Here, now, I feel Thy quiet unhurried power, taking the tension out of my mind and body, and filling me with power. I remember the words, "in quietness and in confidence shall be your strength."

Bless all who are sick, and all who minister Thy healing power. Bless the missionaries of the Church who serve in the uttermost parts of the earth. Give us world peace, that all men shall know one another as brothers, because they know Thee as their God.

As I prepare to sleep, I remember Thy peace, standing guard about the camp of my heart. Amen.

"Now the God of peace, that brought again from the dead our Lord Jesus, that great shepherd of the sheep, through the blood of the everlasting covenant, make you perfect in every good work to do his will, working in you that which is well pleasing in his sight, through Jesus Christ; to whom be glory for ever and ever. Amen." (Hebrews 13:20-21.)

"More Than Conquerors"

BEFORE I ENTERED the room I asked the nurse if this patient knew how seriously ill she was. "Oh, yes," said the nurse with a smile. "She knows she may never be well—but it doesn't worry her! She is in almost constant pain, too, but even pain cannot dull the radiance in her face. That's the reason we who work here, when we feel discouraged ourselves, and need a lift, visit this room. It never fails."

A few minutes later I knew why. I sat before one who had not left her bed for many years. She had known suffering such as few of us experience. She had little hope of recovery. Yet the radiance was there—a joyful acceptance of God's will for her life. She talked of the gracious care of those who ministered to her, and one could see what a joy it was to serve her. Then she talked of the goodness and mercy and love of Him who is the secret of her daily life.

When I left the room after our devotions together I remembered with shame how often I had been impatient and distracted over the petty inconveniences of life. But this woman, who was bearing more suffering than I had ever known, could speak only of the goodness of God and of His people. I had come to the hospital to minister; instead I was ministered unto by one of the Lord's saints.

Though lying helpless on her bed this woman is making her life a daily witness in the Lord's service. The nurses and patients and visitors who come in "for a lift" leave her presence with a new insight into God's love, and a new determination to conquer for Him.

I remembered words of Paul: "Who shall separate us from the love of Christ? shall tribulation, or distress, or persecution . . . ? Nay, in all these things we are more than conquerors through him that loved us." (Romans 8:35, 37.) A strange expression, "more than conquerors." It means that not only have the misfortunes of life no power to conquer our faith, but we can actually make allies of them. We can use tribulation and distress and suffering to teach us more of the love of Christ, and to develop in us radiant Christian lives.

It is not what meets us in life: it is how we meet it that counts.

> " 'Tis the set of a soul
>   That decides its goal,
> And not the calm or the strife."

5

When It Is Hard to Pray

OFTEN during severe illness when we feel we need God most, we find it strangely hard to pray. When I as a pastor visit friends in the sickroom they often say, with disappointment and sometimes with bitterness, "I cannot pray as I want to." Just when it seems that prayer should mean most to us we feel our petitions are rising no higher than the ceiling of our room. Our thoughts begin to wander; worries over trivial things creep into our minds, and we feel like saying with the Ancient Mariner:

> "I looked to heaven and tried to pray;
> But or ever a prayer had gush't
> A wicked whisper came, and made
> My heart as dry as dust."

Let us remember that the physical weakness caused by our illness is often reflected in our minds and spirits. We do not have the powers of mental concentration which are ours when we are well; our emotions are not so easily aroused by the uplift of our devotions. In such times our task is to pray patiently as best we can, and be confident that God hears every sincere petition. As someone has said, "If we cannot pray as we would, then let us pray as we can." The value of prayer does not depend on the warm emotion we "feel," but on God's faithfulness and our sincerity.

It is well in such times to repeat to ourselves short simple prayers and Bible verses, talking to God of our immediate needs. Longer, more formal devotions can be added when strength has returned. Often verses of old hymns can quiet our restless spirits and frame the form of our prayers.

> "My faith looks up to Thee,
>   Thou Lamb of Calvary."

> "Jesus, Thou Joy of loving hearts,
>   Thou Fount of life, Thou Light of men."

> "Dear Lord and Father of mankind,
>   Forgive our foolish ways."

> "Saviour, like a Shepherd lead us,
>   Much we need Thy tender care."

> "O Master, let me walk with Thee
>   In lowly paths of service free."

> "Sun of my soul, Thou Saviour dear,
>   It is not night if Thou be near."

> "O for a closer walk with God,
>   A calm and heavenly frame,
>   A light to shine upon the road
>   That leads me to the Lamb!"

Let us ask, as did the disciples of Jesus long ago, "Lord, teach us to pray."

6

Christian Faith and Today's Tensions

"In quietness and in confidence shall be your strength." (Isaiah 30:15.)

OUR CENTURY has been called the age of speed, but it might better be called the age of hurry. A by-product of the hurry of our age is tension. Americans are the most tense people of the world. Someone has calculated that Americans have 75 per cent of the world's automobiles, 85 per cent of the world's television sets, and use 95 per cent of the world's supply of aspirin and phenobarbital!

Tension takes its toll of physical and mental health. Physicians have learned to control the microbes which cause our diseases, but cannot control the deadly effect of tension on the tissues of our bodies and on our peace of mind. Our tension is also a spiritual problem. As long as the surface of the mind is agitated there can be no deep thoughts of God. We all seem to be in such a hurry—we just *have* to get all these things done! So we become fussily busy people, even bragging about how busy we are. A psychologist has defined such "busy-ness" as a mental illusion cultivated by little people to give themselves a feeling of importance!

One cure for this tension is to think often of Christ, and the calm peace of His life in Galilee. We cannot picture Him as rushed and fretted, dashing feverishly from one appointment to the next. He had time to play with little children, to enjoy the flowers by the wayside, to watch the moonlight's witchery on the waters of Galilee, to walk up into the hills and pray.

> "O Sabbath rest by Galilee,
>   O calm of hills above,
>   Where Jesus knelt to share with Thee
>   The silence of eternity,
>   Interpreted by love!"

Let us remember, also, that God made us to be citizens of two worlds. "One world at a time" is the shallowest motto by which we might live. Every busy day should be transformed by the quiet, patient light of eternity, for we live to praise and serve God forever and ever.

"He that believeth shall not make haste." (Isaiah 28:16.)
"For thus saith the Lord God, the Holy One of Israel; in returning and rest shall ye be saved; in quietness and in confidence shall be your strength." (Isaiah 30:15.)

The Weight of Worry

THE OPPOSITE of faith is worry. Very few people enjoy worrying, but most of us engage in it. It takes a bitter toll of happiness and health. Physicians warn us that the health of our body tissues is affected by our nervous condition.

One woman told her pastor that her husband suffered from gastric ulcers. "Does he worry?" the pastor asked. "Worry?" she replied. "He doesn't do anything else but! Then I got to worrying over his ulcers, and I had a nervous breakdown. Then he worried over my nervous breakdown, and his stomach ulcers got worse!" It is a vicious circle.

It is easy to say "Don't worry" to the other person, but very difficult to take that advice ourselves. We must fill our minds with positive thoughts of God's eternal power and love. Worry is often a refusal to take God at His word, and believe His promises. A deep-seated confidence that God is our loving Heavenly Father strengthens our whole personality for healing.

> "Said the Robin to the Sparrow:
> 'I should really like to know
> Why these anxious human beings
> Rush about and worry so.'

"Said the Sparrow to the Robin:
    'Friend, I think that it must be
That they have no Heavenly Father
    Such as cares for you and me.'"

"God is our refuge and strength, a very present help in trouble." (Psalm 46:1.)

"Have no anxiety about anything, but in everything by prayer and supplication with thanksgiving let your requests be made known to God." (Phillippinas 4:6, R.S.V.)

PRAYER

Heavenly Father, we know that Thou hast made us for Thyself and we are restless till we find rest in Thee. We now ask for an inflowing of Thy Holy Spirit, that every nagging fear and worry may be driven out of our minds. Let Thy peace, which passeth all understanding, stand guard about our hearts and minds.

We pray for the members of our families, for friends, for all who are sick, and for those who minister to us. We pray for our pastor, and for our church. Let Thy blessing of sleep be ours. Through the long watches of this night may the healing power of the Great Physician strengthen the cells of our bodies, that tomorrow may find us moving rapidly toward recovery. In the name of Jesus Christ our Saviour we pray. Amen.

8

Morning—and Worship

" AND GOD SAID, Let there be light: and there was light. And God saw the light, that it was good: and God divided the light from the darkness. And God called the light Day." (Genesis 1 : 3-5.)

"My voice shalt thou hear in the morning, O Lord; in the morning will I direct my prayer unto thee, and will look up." (Psalm 5:3.)

"When I awake, I am still with thee." (Psalm 139:18.)

"Holy, Holy, Holy! Lord God Almighty!
Early in the morning our song shall rise to Thee."

The dawning of each day is the symbol of a new life. For us may it be a day of service, and praise, and fellowship with Him who will walk this way with us. As the east reddens, and the sunlight enters our room, and we worship the Lord . . .

". . . all the jarring notes of life
Seem blending in a psalm,
And all the angles of its strife
Slow rounding into calm.

"And so the shadows fall apart,
And so the west winds play;
And all the windows of my heart
I open to the day."

PRAYER

Creator of the world, and of this new morning, come into my heart and fill it with praise for Thy goodness. I thank Thee for the rest of the night that is past, for the blessing of sleep through the slow watches of the night. I confess unto Thee my sins, that I may begin the day in purity of mind and heart.

Help me daily, Father, to live a more Christlike life in my thoughts, words, and deeds. I pray for Thy blessing upon all who will serve their fellow men this day, especially remembering the physicians and nurses who will minister to my needs. I intercede for others who are suffering. Let the healing of Thy seamless dress be by their beds of pain. Give them of Thy patience and healing power, and return them to their appointed tasks in the service of Thy Kingdom.

I pray for strength to bear pain and weakness with patience and grace, that my life may witness to others of Thy saving power, through Jesus Christ my Redeemer. Amen.

"This is the day which the Lord hath made; we will rejoice and be glad in it." (Psalm 118:24.)

Night—and Sleep

"I will both lay me down in peace, and sleep: for thou, Lord, only makest me dwell in safety." (Psalm 4:8.)

JESUS said: "Come unto me, all ye that labour and are heavy laden, and I will give you rest. Take my yoke upon you, and learn of me; for I am meek and lowly in heart: and ye shall find rest unto your souls. For my yoke is easy, and my burden is light." (Matthew 11:28-30.)

"The darkness and the light are both alike to thee." (Psalm 139:12.)

With faith that God hears our evening prayer, we rest our lives, and all those dear to us, in His keeping. With such confidence filling our thoughts, we can find the blessing of sleep. We remember the faith of David, the Psalmist. When deeply troubled and distressed, he wrote: "I cried unto the Lord with my voice, and he heard me out of his holy hill. I laid me down and slept; I awaked; for the Lord sustained me." (Psalm 3:4-5.)

> "Jesus, give the weary
> Calm and sweet repose;
> With Thy tenderest blessing
> May our eyelids close.

"Through the long night watches,
    May thine angels spread
Their white wings above me,
    Watching round my bed.

"When the morning wakens,
    Then may I arise
Pure, and fresh, and sinless
    In Thy holy eyes."

PRAYER

Loving Father, let Thy quietness and peace steal into my mind and heart. At the close of day the laborers have laid aside their tools. Thy creatures of the wild are resting in their nests and woodland thickets. Thy patient stars move in orderly courses through the night sky. The world of nature renews its strength by Thy gift of rest.

Bless those who serve in hospitals and sickrooms through the long night hours. Grant to doctors and interns, nurses and aides, the reward of joy in Thy service.

Let Thy quiet strength work in my body this night, as I commend myself, and my loved ones, to Thy keeping, through Jesus Christ my Redeemer. Amen.

"He giveth his beloved sleep." (Psalm 127:2.)

10

The Power of Faith

"And God is able to make all grace abound toward you; that ye, always having all sufficiency in all things, may abound to every good work." (II Corinthians 9:8.)

THE INDISPENSABLE element in Christ's miracles of healing was *faith*. Jesus said, "According to your faith be it unto you." (Matthew 9:29.) To the woman who touched His garment in the crowd and found healing, He said, "Be of good comfort; thy faith hath made thee whole." (Matthew 9:22.) He came to one village where the people refused to believe, and we read, "He did not many mighty works there because of their unbelief." (Matthew 13:58.)

There have been many excesses and superstitions which have brought the term "faith healing" into disrepute. It is often associated with those who refuse to use the normal avenues of healing God has given us.

Religious faith is not a substitute for the best medical science we can secure. The two must always work together, for body and soul are a unit. Physicians tell us that the state of our mind and emotions vitally affects our whole body. One physician has said, "The appendix, the gall bladder, the heart, lungs, and other organs are not independent machines, but are linked . . . with a nervous system and with a conscious mind." (Dr. R. C. Cabot of Massachusetts General Hospital.) A deep-seated confidence that God is our Heavenly Father, that His everlasting arms are beneath us and His banner of love is over us, prepares our minds and bodies for healing. Such a faith enables us to relax right on down to the nerves and muscles which control our blood pressure and our digestion.

"A merry heart doeth good like a medicine: but a broken spirit drieth the bones." (Proverbs 17:22.)

"Why art thou cast down, O my soul? and why art thou disquieted within me? hope thou in God: for I shall yet praise him, who is the health of my countenance, and my God." (Psalm 42:11.)

PRAYER

Father, we remember Christ's interest in the sick and pray that Thou wilt increase our faith, that Thy healing power may be able to work in us. We know Thou art able to make all grace abound toward us. May those who minister to us and who visit us this day see the grace and power of the Great Physician reflected in our lives of faith. Through Jesus Christ our Lord. Amen.

He comes to us through faith and prayer,
The Healer, as of old;
We hear His voice, "Arise, and live;
Thy faith hath made thee whole."

11

When Prayer Seems Unanswered

"O Lord, how long shall I cry, and thou wilt not hear!" (Habakkuk 1:2.)

A GODLY MOTHER had a son overseas in the recent war. When the fighting was over and her boy was safe she came to her pastor with joy in her face, saying, "I just knew God was going to spare the life of my son. Every morning and every night I prayed for his life, and God just had to spare him." I have no doubt the prayers of this righteous mother availed much. But even as she talked I thought of thousands of other godly mothers, who prayed just as long and just as earnestly for the lives of their boys, whose sons never came back.

Every one of us knows what it means to pray and apparently to receive no answer. We have prayed for health, and sickness has come. We have prayed at the bedside of some loved one, and perhaps even as we knelt the soul of that dear one slipped its moorings and sailed out into the great unknown. The Bible tells us often that God hears our prayers. Why do so many of them appear unanswered?

Many of our petitions are answered by the loving

Heavenly Father in such a way that we do not recognize His response. Someone has said that often we are asking God for a stone which looks to us like bread, and all the while He is giving us bread which looks to our sinful eyes like a stone!

Jesus in the Garden of Gethsemane earnestly prayed the Father to remove the cup of the Cross. The cup was not removed, but Jesus was given a calm poise which was with Him throughout the ordeal of the crucifixion, as He made atonement for the sins of the world.

Jesus spoke of God as a Father. No earthly father who really loves his children would grant all their foolish requests. Let us ask God for our deepest desires, and then leave Him to answer just when and how His own love for us knows is best.

> "I know not by what methods rare,
> But this I know, God answers prayer.
> I know that He has given His Word,
> Which tells me prayer is always heard,
> And will be answered soon or late,
> And so I pray and calmly wait.
>
> "I know not if the blessing sought
> Will come in just the way I thought;
> But leave my prayers with Him alone,
> Whose will is wiser than my own,
> Assured that He will grant my quest,
> Or send some answer far more blest."

12

"And Be Ye Thankful"

WHEN I WAS recently ill in a hospital in a strange city one verse kept running through my mind—"And God is able to make all grace abound toward you; that ye, always having all sufficiency in all things, may abound to every good work." (II Corinthians 9:8.) Reread the verse, noticing the number of superlatives in that one sentence—"all," "always," "all," "all," "every." If God is ready to do *that* for us, our whole lives should be filled with thankfulness.

As Paul put it once, "Giving thanks unto the Father, which hath made us meet to be partakers of the inheritance of the saints in light: who hath delivered us from the power of darkness, and hath translated us into the kingdom of his dear Son." (Colossians 1:12-13.)

Physicians tell us thanksgiving has real therapeutic value. It concentrates our attention on the things we have, instead of letting us complain and fret for the things we think we lack. A psychologist friend mentioned to me the number of people in a certain mental hospital, and added, "Half are there because they never learned the art of being thankful."

Today, lying on our beds, let us turn our thoughts from

our frustrations and anxieties, and meditate on things for
which we can thank God.

We thank our Heavenly Father:
For the physicians, nurses, hospital aides, and others
ministering to us.
For hospital, bed, medicines, food and drink.
For the beauty of flowers at our bedside, or the glimpse
of tree and sky from our window.
For human love of family and friends surrounding us.
For the certainty of a Heavenly Father's care, that His
everlasting arms are beneath us, and His banner of love
over us.
For quiet meditation on the life of Christ, His calm peace,
His healing power.
For the values we can gain from our pain and hardships.
For the certainty of life everlasting in the Father's care.

"Be thankful unto him, and bless his name. For the Lord
is good; his mercy is everlasting; and his truth endureth to
all generations." (Psalm 100:4-5.)
"And let the peace of God rule in your hearts, to the
which also ye are called in one body; *and be ye thankful.*"
(Colossians 3:15.)

13

Accidents—and the Plan of God

THERE ARE TIMES when each of us asks, "Why should this misfortune happen to me?" "Why was it necessary for me to suffer this disease or accident?" Sometimes we know we suffer ill health because we have failed to take care of the temples of our bodies. Sin is not only morally bad; it is also unhealthy. We sin not only against God; sin reacts against our nervous systems, our hearts, our digestive tracts.

But many accidents and diseases come through no fault of ours. When the disciples saw a man who was blind from his birth they asked, "Master, who did sin, this man, or his parents, that he was born blind?" Jesus answered, "Neither hath this man sinned, nor his parents: but that the works of God should be made manifest in him." (John 9:3.) Some of the best people suffer most, and we cannot refrain from asking, "Why?"

God has not revealed to us all His plan for our lives. The Bible tells us God's ways are not our ways, and His thoughts are not our thoughts.

"Not until the loom is silent
And the shuttles cease to fly

> Will God unroll the canvas
> And explain the reason why;
>
> "How the dark threads are as needful,
> In the weaver's skillful hand,
> As the threads of gold and silver
> In the pattern He has planned."

But of this we can be sure: back of this universe is not a blind chance, but an all-powerful Father. He has a plan for our lives, and nothing we call accident can defeat the plan of Almighty God. Jesus said, "Are not two sparrows sold for a farthing? and one of them shall not fall on the ground without your Father. . . . ye are of more value than many sparrows." (Matthew 10:29, 31.)

"And we know that all things work together for good to them that love God, to them who are the called according to his purpose." (Romans 8:28.)

PRAYER

Father, we do not understand all Thy purpose for our life, why pain and sorrow and frustration should be a part of it. We do know that Thou art our Loving Father. Give us faith so to accept each trial that we may grow into the likeness of Him who was made perfect through suffering, even Jesus Christ our Lord. Amen.

14

The Ministry of Service

"For even the Son of man came not to be ministered unto, but to minister, and to give his life a ransom for many." (Mark 10:45.)

THOSE who give themselves to the ministry of healing in their service of the Great Physician merit our honor and appreciation. We remember the skill and devotion of physicians, who through long years of exacting discipline have prepared themselves for their service. We rejoice in the new insights into the human mind and body, and honor the scientists who in their laboratories have produced new drugs with amazing healing power.

We know the efficient service of the nurses, with the taxing demands made upon them daily. We find something of the patient care of the Great Physician Himself expressed through their ministering hands.

There are others who minister in hospitals—student nurses and nurses' aides, orderlies, and a host of others we never see—administrators and supervisors, technicians and cooks, maids and janitors. There are loved ones who minister to the sick and shut-ins at home.

The helplessness of sickness, when we are utterly dependent on others for our most trivial needs, teaches us that all of God's children are bound together in mutual de-dependence upon one another, and upon him.

We should be humbly grateful for the service of others.

We should seek to be worthy of the care we receive.

We should find ways, even while ill, to spread comfort and cheer to those we meet each day. By our cheerful acceptance of our lot, our gracious appreciation of service received, our calm trust in the Great Physician, we in our illness can witness daily to the power of God in our lives.

As loved ones minister to us at home we should resolve to bring more unselfishness and patience and love into our family life.

We should dedicate ourselves to lives of service, in Christ's name.

PRAYER

Father, we thank Thee that Thou dost call consecrated men and women to be doctors and nurses and other helpers in the ministry of healing. May they find strength, patience, and joy in their service. Help me this day, I pray, by some word or deed, to shed abroad to others my faith in Thee. Through Christ our Lord. Amen.

15

When God Does Not Seem Real to Us

"Oh that I knew where I might find him!" (Job 23:3.)

TO EACH OF US there come times when God does not seem real, when our Bible reading leaves us cold, and when our prayers seem futile—when holiness has lost its thrill and God seems to be far away from us. We remember the promise in God's Word, "Lo, I am with you alway, even unto the end of the world." (Matthew 28:20.) We think of the chorus we used to sing, "He walks with me and He talks with me." Why is God not real to us now?

Perhaps we have reduced our personal devotional life to a cold, formal routine, as dead as Ezekiel's valley of dry bones. Or worse, we may have let other things crowd out our devotions completely. Someone has said that instead of listening to God's Word, "Be still, and know that I am God," we ask God to listen to us—and we say, "Wait a minute, God, I must answer the telephone"! How high a priority are we giving God in our daily schedule?

Perhaps some sin harbored in our hearts has dimmed the

reality of God. Jesus said, "Blessed are the pure in heart: for *they* shall see God." (Matthew 5:8.) Sometimes we want God, but we do not want Him in all of our lives. We want to reserve one little corner for our own selfishness. We are afraid if we get too religious we may miss something in life, so we hold back a little of ourselves to have a good time with, and do not give ourselves completely to Him. We must remember, "Ye shall seek me, and find me, when ye shall search for me with all your heart." (Jeremiah 29:13.)

One night a man dreamed that Christ came to him and said, "Give me the keys to your heart." The man took out his keys—keys related to his home, his work, his pleasures. But the key to one small inner room he felt he could not give up. Thinking Christ would not miss that one tiny key, he removed it and handed over the rest. The Master put them all back upon the table, and gently said, "Give me the key to that inner room, too. I must have all—or none."

PRAYER

God, I know that far more important than my seeking for Thee, is Thy seeking for me. Now, in this moment, I open all the doors of my heart to Thee.

> "Into my heart, into my heart,
> Come into my heart, Lord Jesus;
> Come in today, come in to stay,
> Come into my heart, Lord Jesus. Amen."

16

The Art of Contentment

"For I have learned, in whatsoever state I am, therewith to be content." (Philippians 4:11.)

THIS IS an amazing statement which Paul made, for the word he used for "learn" means to learn out of one's own experience. Paul's life had not been one of calm security and quiet prosperity. He wrote his autobiography in the words, "In labours more abundant, in stripes above measure, in prisons more frequent, in deaths oft . . . in weariness and painfulness, in watchings often, in hunger and thirst, in fastings often, in cold and nakedness." (II Corinthians 11:23, 27.) When he wrote that he had learned how to be content he was in a Roman prison, waiting to stand trial for his life before the despot Nero.

Certainly Paul was a master of the art of contentment. His secret was living daily in the light of the greatest truths he knew. He faced his worries and fears with the most significant facts his mind could comprehend.

The art of contentment is meeting life in the light of the greatest truth we know about God—His sovereign love. This world is not controlled by unthinking luck or crazy chance, but by a merciful Father. We can meet every worry and fear with the knowledge that the eternal God is our refuge, and underneath are the everlasting arms. (Deuteronomy 33:27.)

We can meet life with the greatest truth we know about ourselves—that we are children of God. We are more than bodies subject to the vicissitudes of daily existence. We are immortal spirits with a destiny beyond the stars. We meet each day in the light of God's plan for us through the eternal ages, so that the quiet radiance of eternity may transform every mundane hour.

To live daily in the light of the greatest truths we know about God and His will for us is to find the art of contentment. We can learn to say, out of our own experience, "I have learned, in whatsoever state I am, therewith to be content."

PRAYER

God, in the midst of the discomfort, frustration, and even resentment which illness often brings, we pray for quiet contentment and peace. We would leave the reasons for it all in Thine eternal love and grace, and pray now for that measure of Thy Spirit we need for today. Look into our hearts, see the deep needs which in us lie, and answer those needs according to Thy riches in glory in Christ Jesus our Lord. Amen.

17

"Fear Not"

TIME AND TIME AGAIN, Jesus spoke such words as these during the years of His ministry: "Be not afraid"; "Fear not, little flock; for it is your Father's good pleasure to give you the kingdom"; "Why are ye fearful, O ye of little faith?" (Mark 5:36; Luke 12:32; Matthew 8:26.)

Fear springs from the unknown. Faith shows us that "behind the dim unknown, standeth God within the shadow, keeping watch above His own."

Once during a severe storm at sea all the passengers of the ship were terrified, save one little girl, who walked calm and unafraid about the deck. When someone asked, "Why aren't you afraid?" she replied, "My father is the captain of this ship."

"The Lord is my light and my salvation; whom shall I fear? the Lord is the strength of my life; of whom shall I be afraid? . . . Though an host should encamp against me, my heart shall not fear." (Psalm 27:1, 3.)

PRAYER

Eternal God, Thou art our Father, we are Thy children, and we praise Thy Holy Name. We confess unto Thee our sins, and ask for Thy forgiveness through the atonement made by Christ on the cross. Give us the joy and peace which come when we know that as far as the east is from the west, so far hast Thou removed our transgressions from us.

We thank Thee for friends and loved ones who have expressed their interest and love this day. We pray for all who are hungry and cold, for all who needlessly suffer through lack of medical care, for all who have not found Christ as Saviour.

At the close of this day we give ourselves to Thy service and love, till the day comes when in Thine infinite mercy we shall become a part of the great General Assembly of the redeemed, singing praises about the throne of the Lamb of God. In His name we pray. Amen.

"For God hath not given us the spirit of fear; but of power, and of love, and of a sound mind." (II Timothy 1:7.)

"When thou liest down, thou shalt not be afraid: yea, thou shalt lie down, and thy sleep shall be sweet." (Proverbs 3:24.)

"Fear not, I am with thee, O be not dismayed,
　For I am thy God, and will still give thee aid;
　I'll strengthen thee, help thee, and cause thee to stand,
　Upheld by My righteous, omnipotent hand."

18

Glorifying God

"My strength is made perfect in weakness." (II Corinthians 12:9.)

WHAT IS THE PURPOSE of our lives? Why are we here anyway? A well-known church creed (Westminster Shorter Catechism) begins with the question, "What is the chief end of man?" The answer is, "Man's chief end is to glorify God, and to enjoy Him forever."

We glorify God by performing courageous acts of service to our fellow men, by leadership in the church and state. But we can also glorify Him by patience in pain, by faith in the midst of suffering, by calm poise and quiet faith during illness. Who knows but in God's sight the greatest service we ever render is the way we bear our afflictions, the quiet word of patience we speak from our sickbed, the smile of faith from our pillow.

Robert Louis Stevenson wrote to a friend, "For fourteen years I have not had a day of real health. I have wakened sick, and gone to bed weary. I have written my books in bed and out of bed, written them between hemorrhages, written them when I was torn by coughing, written them when my head swam from weakness . . . But the battle still goes on. . . . I was made for a contest, and the Powers That Be have willed that my battlefield shall be the dingy inglorious one of the bed and medicine bottle." (Letter to George Meredith, 1893.)

Paul tells us of a physical infirmity he had, which he called his "thorn in the flesh." He tells us that three times he prayed God to remove it, but instead God answered Paul, "My grace is sufficient for thee: for my strength is made perfect in weakness." Then Paul added, "Most gladly therefore will I rather glory in my infirmities, that the power of Christ may rest upon me. . . . for when I am weak, then am I strong." (II Corinthians 12:7-10.)

In our sickness and pain and weakness the strength of Christ may be made perfect, and God glorified.

PRAYER

Father, we do not know why these "thorns in the flesh" are sent to trouble us. But we pray for Thy grace that we may win the battle over frustration, self-pity, and despair, and find the power of Christ made strong in us. May our chief end during these days be to meet our infirmities with such courage, faith, and patience that Thy name may be glorified in us. Amen.

19

Enjoying God

"Rejoice in the Lord alway: and again I say, Rejoice."
(Philippians 4:4.)

"These things have I spoken unto you, that my joy might remain in you, and that your joy might be full." (John 15:11.)

THE ANSWER to the first question in the Shorter Catechism is, "Man's chief end is to glorify God, and to enjoy Him forever." That last phrase suggests that a part of our chief end in life is to "enjoy God." We are not only to serve Him, and glorify His name by our righteous living; we are to enjoy Him! If God is not the greatest source of joy in our lives, something is wrong with us.

Dwight Moody said he was once walking down the street, thinking of how good God was to him. He said he became so happy as he walked that at each step one foot seemed to shout, "Glory to God," and the other to answer, "Hallelujah!" Too often we have made our faith a drab, somber, gloomy matter. Billy Sunday used to complain that some Christians had faces so long they could eat oatmeal out of a gas pipe! No wonder men have hesitated to become

Christians, for fear it would spoil their happiness in life! How different was Jesus, who found His highest joy in His Heavenly Father.

During these quiet days when our illness is forcing us to rest we can meditate on the glorious truths of God's care for us. Worries come because we are taking the trouble in the world more seriously than the greatness of God. On our sickbeds we can find opportunity to let others see the joy of our Lord radiating from our faces. Anyone can be happy when everything is fine. Perhaps it is a real test of our faith to show our joy when pain and frustration and sorrow afflict us.

"Rejoice in the Lord always."

Robert Louis Stevenson, when ill with tuberculosis, his throat torn with incessant coughing, wrote this prayer:

> "If I have faltered more or less
> In my great task of happiness;
> If I have moved among my race
> And shown no glorious morning face;
> If beams from happy human eyes
> Have moved me not; if morning skies,
> Books, and my food, and summer rain
> Knocked on my sullen heart in vain:—
> Lord, Thy most pointed pleasure take
> And stab my spirit broad awake."

20

"I Believe . . . in the Life Everlasting"

"LET NOT your heart be troubled: ye believe in God, believe also in me. In my Father's house are many mansions: if it were not so, I would have told you. I go to prepare a place for you. And if I go and prepare a place for you, I will come again, and receive you unto myself; that where I am, there ye may be also." (John 14:1-3.)

"Because I live, ye shall live also." (John 14:19.)

"I am the resurrection, and the life: he that believeth in me, though he were dead, yet shall he live: and whosoever liveth and believeth in me shall never die." (John 11:25-26.)

"The Lord is my shepherd; I shall not want. . . . Yea, though I walk through the valley of the shadow of death, I will fear no evil: for thou art with me; thy rod and thy staff they comfort me." (Psalm 23:1, 4.)

"For we know that if our earthly house of this tabernacle were dissolved, we have a building of God, an house not made with hands, eternal in the heavens." (II Corinthians 5:1.)

"I know not what the future hath
        Of marvel or surprise,
Assured alone that life and death
        His mercy underlies.

.   .   .   .

"And so beside the Silent Sea
        I wait the muffled oar;
No harm from Him can come to me
        On ocean or on shore.

"I know not where His islands lift
        Their fronded palms in air;
I only know I cannot drift
        Beyond His love and care."

PRAYER

We thank Thee, Father, that Thou art the Lord of death, as well as of life. We know Thou hast made us to be citizens of two worlds, and believe that some day Thou wilt lead us through the gates the world calls death, into the morn that shall tearless be. We thank Thee for the death and resurrection of Christ. Because He lives, we know we shall live also, for Thou hast planned for us an eternity of service and fellowship in the mansions of the Heavenly Father, through the Christ, our crucified and risen Redeemer. Amen.

"When by His grace I shall look on His face,
        That will be glory for me."

21

The Healer—at Evening Time

"BUT SIMON'S wife's mother lay sick of a fever, and anon they tell him of her. And he came and took her by the hand, and lifted her up; and immediately the fever left her, and she ministered unto them. And at even, when the sun did set, they brought unto him all that were diseased, and them that were possessed with devils. And all the city was gathered together at the door. And he healed many that were sick of divers diseases." (Mark 1:30-34.)

"At even, when the sun was set,
The sick, O Lord, around Thee lay;
O in what divers pains they met!
O with what joy they went away!

"Once more 'tis eventide, and we,
Oppressed with various ills, draw near:
What if Thy form we cannot see?
We know and feel that Thou art here.

. . . .

"O Saviour Christ, Thou too art man;
Thou hast been troubled, tempted, tried;
Thy kind but searching glance can scan
The very wounds that shame would hide.

"Thy touch has still its ancient power,
No word from Thee can fruitless fall:
Hear in this solemn evening hour,
And in Thy mercy heal us all."

"For we have not an high priest which cannot be touched with the feeling of our infirmities; but was in all points tempted like as we are, yet without sin. Let us therefore come boldly unto the throne of grace, that we may obtain mercy, and find grace to help in time of need." (Hebrews 4:15-16.)

PRAYER

Father, Thou hast made the night with its quietness and rest to follow the activity of the day. We now put aside every distressing burden to sleep in quiet forgetfulness, remembering only that Thou with Thy healing power art with us, nearer than breathing, closer than hands and feet. Through Jesus Christ our Lord. Amen.

"The Lord bless thee, and keep thee:
The Lord make his face shine upon thee, and be gracious unto thee:
The Lord lift up his countenance upon thee, and give thee peace." (Numbers 6:24-26.)

The Art of Growing Old

"They that wait upon the Lord shall renew their strength." (Isaiah 40:31.)

EVERY ONE OF US is engaged in the process of growing older. Some look upon it with dread, assuming that youth is the secret of happiness. But wiser men have realized that God made us for the latter part of life, too, and it can be the most satisfying and worth-while time of all. As George MacDonald said, "Age is not decay; it is the ripening, the swelling of the fresh life within."

There are dangers in growing old which we must carefully avoid. There is the danger of losing interest in things.

"For this thing humbly would I pray:
O Lord, let not my soul grow gray."

There is the danger of fear of change, living in the "good old days" which are gone forever. There is the danger that we shall become too sensitive to real or imagined slights, and grow self-centered and narrow. These dangers we must avoid.

But there are joys peculiar to old age. There are the blessings of memories. How well to cultivate the motto on the sundial, "I count only sunny hours." There is the value of experience, which we can apply to the needs of every day. There are opportunities for new experiences, to cultivate new hobbies, to find new satisfactions. Victor Hugo once wrote, "Winter is on my head, but spring is in my heart."

The joys of God's service and worship are for every age, but the mature Christian with long experience can plumb a depth of satisfaction the youth cannot know. May we so live that we can say with Rabbi Ben Ezra:

> "Grow old along with me!
>   The best is yet to be,
>   The last of life, for which the first was made:
>   Our times are in His hand
>   Who saith 'A whole I planned,
>   Youth shows but half; trust God: see all, nor
>   be afraid!' "

PRAYER

> "God keep my heart attuned to laughter
>   When youth is done;
>   When all the days are gray days, coming after
>   The warmth, the sun.
>   God keep me then from bitterness, from grieving,
>   When life seems cold;
>   God keep me always loving and believing
>   As I grow old."

23

"Forgive Us Our Debts"

"If we confess our sins, he is faithful and just to forgive us our sins, and to cleanse us from all unrighteousness." (I John 1:9.)

ONE NEED every one of us has is for forgiveness. All of us know the burning pangs of remorse—"Why did I do that thing?" "What possessed me to say that careless word?" "Why did I let that opportunity for service pass unused?" The most common worry we have is the burden of guilt. "If we say that we have no sin, we deceive ourselves, and the truth is not in us." (I John 1:8.)

The Christian faith has answer for our guilt. It never says sin does not matter. It does not teach us to blame someone else, as Adam did ("The woman whom thou gavest to be with me"). It does not foolishly teach us just to forget it. It does not ask us to grow morbid in our worries over past transgressions. Rather, it teaches us to repent of our sins.

There are five elementary steps in repentance.

First, we *recognize* the sin in us. We should examine our hearts to see the sins of omission and commission, of thought, word, and deed. We see our own evil in contrast with Christ's perfection.

Second, we repent by honestly *confessing* to God.

Third, we *resolve* that with God's help we shall commit this sin no more. Confession has no value if we have a sneaking suspicion in the bottom of our minds that we are going out and commit the same sin again!

Fourth, we make *restitution,* by correcting as best we can the evils we have done.

Fifth, we experience the glorious *release* when we know our sins are forgiven. Christ died on the cross for our sins, in some way we cannot understand making atonement for us. "Who his own self bare our sins in his own body on the tree." (I Peter 2:24.) So we can take our burdens to the Lord, and leave them there.

PRAYER

Let us silently confess our sins to God.
Let us meditate on the promises of His forgiveness.

"Come now, and let us reason together, saith the Lord: though your sins be as scarlet, they shall be as white as snow; though they be red like crimson, they shall be as wool." (Isaiah 1:18.)

"As far as the east is from the west, so far hath he removed our transgressions from us." (Psalm 103:12.)

"And that repentance and remission of sins should be preached in his name among all nations." (Luke 24:47.)

"Neither do I condemn thee: go, and sin no more." (John 8:11.)

Glorying in Tribulation

"We glory in tribulations also: knowing that tribulation worketh patience; and patience, experience; and experience, hope: and hope maketh not ashamed; because the love of God is shed abroad in our hearts by the Holy Ghost which is given unto us." (Romans 5:3-5.)

"My son, despise not thou the chastening of the Lord, nor faint when thou art rebuked of him: for whom the Lord loveth he chasteneth, and scourgeth every son whom he receiveth." (Hebrews 12:5-6.)

PAIN, suffering, and hardship can strengthen the moral fibers of our souls if we will properly meet them in our lives. Men have become truly great, not because they were free from all the pains and sorrows of life, but because they used their very hardships to strengthen their characters.

The final answer to the problem of suffering is the cross. Christ lived the one sinless life; yet He suffered, beyond our comprehension. We are told that He was made "perfect through sufferings." (Hebrews 2:10.) When we find something of the cross in our own experience, let us seek grace to use it as God's plan for growth into Christ-likeness.

A legend is told of a youth who went with an old violin maker into the forest to cut wood for violins. They passed through the fertile valley, and went high on the crags of the mountain's side, where gnarled and knotty trunks were twisted by the gales. The boy asked why they had not stopped in the protected valley below, where the trees grew straight and tall. The old violin maker explained how the wood which grew up quickly in the sheltered valley would break under the strain of being made into violins; but the trees that all their lives had been lashed and torn by the gales were tough, and when carved into violins made the sweetest music. That night, as the boy lay in bed, he listened to the fierce storms tearing and lashing at the trees on the mountainside, and knew that their fibers were being strengthened and toughened to make the sweetest music of all.

"Now no chastening for the present seemeth to be joyous, but grievous: nevertheless afterward it yieldeth the peaceable fruit of righteousness unto them which are exercised thereby." (Hebrews 12:11.)

25

"Think on These Things"

ILLNESS often brings long days when we are shut off from our usual employments and recreations, sometimes with a "no visitors" sign outside our door. Through the long hours of the day, and in the quiet watches of the night when sleep eludes us, what shall we think about?

"Finally, brethren, whatsover things are true, whatsoever things are honest, whatsoever things are just, whatsoever things are pure, whatsoever things are lovely, whatsoever things are of good report; if there be any virtue, and if there be any praise, think on these things." (Philippians 4:8.)

"For as he thinketh in his heart, so is he." (Proverbs 23:7.)

"Blessed are the pure in heart: for they shall see God." (Matthew 5:8.)

I will search my heart, and confess my sins to God, and rest in His forgiveness.

I will fill my mind with thanksgiving for those who minister to me.

I will not cease to marvel at the wonders of the world God has made, at the intricate mechanism of my own body, and at the miracle of healing.

I will think often of the ministry of my Lord in the days of His flesh, and plan my own service for others.

In these days of enforced quiet I will be still and know that the Lord is God.

> "Drop Thy still dews of quietness,
>   Till all our strivings cease;
> Take from our souls the strain and stress,
> And let our ordered lives confess
>   The beauty of Thy peace."

"To get peace, if you want it, make for yourselves nests of pleasant thoughts. . . . Bright fancies, satisfied memories, noble histories, faithful sayings, treasure houses of precious and restful thoughts which care cannot disturb, nor pain make gloomy, nor poverty take away from us—houses built without hands, for our souls to live in." (John Ruskin.)

"Thou wilt keep him in perfect peace, whose mind is stayed on thee: because he trusteth in thee." (Isaiah 26:3.)

"Search me, O God, and know my heart: try me, and know my thoughts: and see if there be any wicked way in me, and lead me in the way everlasting." (Psalm 139:23-24.)

The Gates of Pearl

RECENTLY a friend who has been very ill with a painful disease said to his pastor, "I am a better person because of this suffering." His daily life during his convalescence is already showing that he has learned how to use pain and difficulty for his spiritual growth.

Every one of us meets in life enough hardships to crush us, unless we learn how to meet and use them. Truly great souls are those who have used for good the very difficulties which left others discouraged and broken.

Old Epictetus was a slave, and crippled, and never free from pain, but he made of life a wonderful thing. Louis Pasteur was crippled by a paralytic stroke. Milton was blind; Beethoven was deaf; Helen Keller became deaf and blind while still a small child. But each conquered these handicaps to become great souls. Someone has said that in God's army only wounded soldiers can serve.

In the book of Revelation there is a vision of the City of God, the New Jerusalem, with its twelve gates. Each gate is a pearl. Do you remember how pearls are made? Some little shellfish is wounded; perhaps a grain of sand or bit of stone lodges in the tender living tissue of that creature.

Slowly and quietly the life processes heal that hurt, and after a long time instead of an ugly wound there is a pearl, one of the loveliest creations of nature. The gates leading into the City of God are pearls. It is with pains and wounds and hardships that we are prepared to enter the Kingdom of Glory.

PRAYER

Great Physician, may I find a high adventure in meeting the hardships and disappointments of life. Give me courage to use everything which comes to me to grow into the likeness of Christ. If something of the cross should be my lot, may I remember the One who was made perfect through suffering, Jesus Christ my Redeemer. Amen.

"And we know that all things work together for good to them that love God, to them who are the called according to his purpose." (Romans 8:28.)

Troubled Waters

ONE OF THE VALUES which suffering brings is teaching us how to comfort others in need. Only those who have themselves really suffered can minister to others in deep distress.

Thornton Wilder has a playlet entitled, "The Angel That Troubled the Waters." In it he imagines that at the pool of Bethesda in old Jerusalem was a man praying that God would send healing to his body. At last the angel came down to trouble the waters. But the angel told the man that healing was not for him. His task was to bear comfort to others in pain and anguish.

The angel said, "The very angels themselves cannot persuade the wretched and blundering children on earth as can one human being broken on the wheels of living. In Love's service only the wounded soldiers can serve. Draw back." Then the angel reached down and troubled the waters. The sufferer drew back, while someone else hobbled into the pool and was healed. Then, as the sufferer was standing there like a statue of grief, thinking of what might have been, an old neighbor approached him and said, "May you be the next, my brother. But come with me first, an hour only, to my home. My son is lost in dark thoughts.

I—I do not understand him, and only you have ever lifted his mood. Only an hour . . . my daughter since her child has died, sits in the shadow. She will not listen to us. . . ."

"In Love's service only the wounded soldiers can serve."

"Blessed is the man whom thou chastenest, O Lord, and teachest him out of thy law." (Psalm 94:12.)

"As many as I love, I rebuke and chasten." (Revelation 3:19.)

"Blessed be God, even the Father of our Lord Jesus Christ, the Father of mercies, and the God of all comfort; who comforteth us in all our tribulation, that we may be able to comfort them which are in any trouble, by the comfort wherewith we ourselves are comforted of God." (II Corinthians 1:3-4.)

PRAYER

Let us pray for all in this hospital in pain, or worry, or fear . . . . .

Let us pray for all who minister here—nurses, physicians, aides, orderlies, cooks, maids . . . . .

Let us pray for our family . . . . .

Let us pray for others in special need . . . sickness . . . bereaved . . . facing difficult decisions . . . tempted . . . . .

Let us pray for ourselves, that we may use this our illness for our growth in God's grace . . . . .

Let us pray for Christians in difficult parts of the world, persecuted for their faith . . . . .

Let us pray for the peace of the world . . . . .

28

Dedication of Life

"For God so loved the world, that he gave his only begotten Son, that whosoever believeth in him should not perish, but have everlasting life." (John 3:16.)

"Therefore if any man be in Christ, he is a new creature: old things are passed away; behold, all things are become new." (II Corinthians 5:17.)

WHILE we are recovering from illness and are especially thankful for God's goodness, it is a good time to dedicate ourselves to our Lord.

Some who read these pages have never accepted Christ as Saviour. Jesus calls us to confess humbly our sins, and to rest for salvation in His redeeming grace. You will want to notify the minister of the church of your choice about your decision, and make your profession of faith, joining in the fellowship of God's people.

"If thou shalt confess with thy mouth the Lord Jesus, and shalt believe in thine heart that God hath raised him from the dead, thou shalt be saved. . . . For whosoever shall call upon the name of the Lord shall be saved." (Romans 10:9, 13.)

Others of us have long been Christians, but as we recover from our illness we would dedicate ourselves to finer service, more genuine worship, and more unselfish Christian living. We will leave the old life behind, with the disease and pain, with its sinful habits. We will rise from our beds in newness of life, better servants of the King.

"If ye then be risen with Christ, seek those things which are above." (Colossians 3 : 1.)

PRAYER

Lord, I humbly confess unto Thee my sins. I confess particularly the sin of this . . . and this . . . and of this sinful habit . . . I pray for Thy forgiveness, not because of any merit in myself, but because of the atonement made by Christ on the cross. He died for me.

I dedicate my life anew to Thee. Take me, and use me as Thy servant. As I return to my daily walk of life I pledge myself, by the power of Thy Spirit, to live under Thy guidance, in the service of my fellow men, for the glory of my Redeemer and King, in whose name I pray. Amen.

> "Just as I am, without one plea
> But that Thy blood was shed for me,
> And that Thou bidd'st me come to Thee
> O Lamb of God, I come!
>
> "Just as I am, Thou wilt receive,
> Wilt welcome, pardon, cleanse, relieve;
> Because Thy promise I believe,
> O Lamb of God, I come!"

Thanksgiving for Recovery

Merciful God, I thank Thee that Thy power has sustained me during the days of my illness, and that the healing of the Great Physician is mine. I praise Thy Holy Name for Thy goodness to me, for Thy love and peace which were mine during the days of pain and discomfort.

I thank Thee for those who have ministered to me, and I would now seek to live worthy of their service.

Give me patience during these days of convalescence. May I wait in calmness for the return of health and strength. Keep my mind from the sin of impatience if recovery seems slow.

Guide me, Father, as I take up once more the ordinary threads of life in home, business, and community. I resolve to live in newness of life, leaving behind with the conquered disease the old sinful habits, and giving myself to a pure and joyous fellowship in Thy Kingdom. Because I have been ministered unto, I will now seek ways to minister to others in need, through Jesus Christ our Lord. Amen.

The Twenty-third Psalm

The Lord is my shepherd; I shall not want. He maketh me to lie down in green pastures: he leadeth me beside the still waters. He restoreth my soul: he leadeth me in the paths of righteousness for his name's sake.

Yea, though I walk through the valley of the shadow of death, I will fear no evil: for thou art with me; thy rod and thy staff they comfort me.

Thou preparest a table before me in the presence of mine enemies: thou anointest my head with oil; my cup runneth over. Surely goodness and mercy shall follow me all the days of my life: and I will dwell in the house of the Lord for ever.

THE DOXOLOGY

"Praise God from whom all blessings flow;
Praise Him, all creatures here below;
Praise Him above, ye heavenly host:
Praise Father, Son, and Holy Ghost. Amen."

Acknowledgments

The Divine Physician

"But warm, sweet, tender, even yet" . . . . from "Immortal Love, Forever Full," by John Greenleaf Whittier.

The Power of Prayer

"More things are wrought by prayer" . . . . from "Morte D'Arthur," by Alfred, Lord Tennyson.

Peace Standing Guard

"In quietness and in confidence" . . . . from Isaiah 30:15.

"More Than Conquerors"

" 'Tis the set of a soul" . . . . from "The Winds of Fate," by Ella Wheeler Wilcox.

When It Is Hard to Pray

"I looked to heaven and tried to pray" . . . . from "Rime of the Ancient Mariner," by Samuel Taylor Coleridge.

Christian Faith and Today's Tensions

"O Sabbath rest by Galilee" . . . . from "Dear Lord and Father of Mankind," by John Greenleaf Whittier.

The Weight of Worry

"Said the Robin to the Sparrow" . . . . "Overheard in an Orchard," by Elizabeth Cheney. From *Masterpieces of Religious Verse,* Harper & Brothers. By permission.

Philippians 4:6. Quoted from The Revised Standard Version of the Holy Bible. Copyright by Division of Christian Education of the National Council of the Churches of Christ in the United States of America.

Morning—and Worship

Lines from "Holy, Holy, Holy!" by Bishop Reginald Heber.

". . . all the jarring notes of life" . . . . from "My Psalm," by John Greenleaf Whittier.

Night—and Sleep

Lines from "Now the Day Is Over," by Rev. Sabine Baring-Gould.

The Power of Faith

Statement by Dr. Cabot is quoted from *The Art of Ministering to the Sick,* by Richard C. Cabot, M.D., and Russell L. Dicks, B.D. (p. 6). The Macmillan Company.

"He comes to us through faith and prayer" . . . . by William B. Ward.

When Our Prayer Is Not Answered

"I know not by what methods rare" . . . . "This I Know," by Eliza M. Hickok.

Accidents—and the Plan of God

"Not until the loom is silent" . . . . by an unknown author.

When God Does Not Seem Real to Us

Story of a dream adapted from F. B. Meyer.

"Fear Not"

"Behind the dim unknown" . . . . from "The Present Crisis," by James Russell Lowell.

"Fear not, I am with thee" . . . . from "How Firm a Foundation," by "K" in Rippon's *Selection,* 1787.

Enjoying God

"If I have faltered more or less" . . . . from "The Celestial Surgeon," by Robert Louis Stevenson.

"I Believe . . . in the Life Everlasting"

"I know not what the future hath" . . . . from "The Eternal Goodness," by John Greenleaf Whittier.

"When by His grace" . . . . from "O That Will Be Glory," by Charles H. Gabriel.

The Healer—at Evening Time
  Stanza from "At Even, When the Sun Was Set," by Rev. Henry Twells.

The Art of Growing Old
  "For this thing humbly would I pray . . ." Source unknown.
  "Grow old along with me!" . . . . from "Rabbi Ben Ezra," by Robert Browning.
  "God keep my heart attuned to laughter" . . . . from "As I Grow Old," by an unknown author.

"Think on These Things"
  "Drop Thy still dews of quietness" . . . . from "Dear Lord and Father of Mankind," by John Greenleaf Whittier.
  "To get peace, if you want it" . . . . from *The Eagle's Nest,* by John Ruskin, paragraph 205. First sentence slightly adapted.

Troubled Waters
  Excerpts from *The Angel That Troubled the Waters and Other Plays,* by Thornton Wilder. Copyright, 1928, by Coward-McCann, Inc. Used by permission.

Dedication of Life
  Stanzas from "Just as I Am," by Charlotte Elliott.